Broken to Built

31 Days of Rebuilding with Nehemiah

Barry Pearman

Barry Pearman

Copyright © 2018 Barry Pearman. All rights reserved.

The information contained within this book may not be reproduced in any material form or transmitted to any persons without permission from Barry Pearman under the Copyright Act 1994.

ISBN:9781717829702

Scripture version used

World English Version

CONTENTS

INTRODUCTION

Once upon a time we lived in a far faraway home called Eden, but now we are in recovery mode. We are building and growing a life out of the rubble of what was left behind. In the choking dust of rubble we find that this is no fairy tale.

The biblical Book of Nehemiah is a love story. God is in love with the people of Jerusalem and sees them broken, shamed and without dignity.

This is not a story of fairy godmothers, magic wands and quick-fix solutions. This is not a first-aid tent applying bandages that will fall off, given friction.

Recovery for the people of Jerusalem was relentlessly hard work. There was criticism and scoffing, alluring distractions and fatigue.

In the pages ahead I have sifted out some thoughts about recovery from the story of Nehemiah.

The big idea is that recovery or life takes place in a relational context. We have others next to us. As you will discover, this is a story of people like you and me. It's a story of a community of people like us gathering around a fragile broken heart. Most of the community are helpful in the rebuild, but some not, and in fact some will be totally against the change.

To get the most out of this book, treat it like a friend who is but a few steps ahead of you and shouts back, 'Hey, this is what I've learnt'.

Read it with a friend or two. Discuss the questions and notice thoughts that spring up seemingly from nowhere. Jot them down, ponder over them and see where they lead.

Take your time and chip your way through the book.

Barry Pearman

History and characters of the story

Before we dive into the story, we need to understand some of the background and some of the key players.

In December 589 B.C. the Babylonian King Nebuchadnezzar began a siege of Jerusalem (2 Kings 25:1; Ezekiel 24:1–2). He installed Zedekiah to be King of Judah but Zedekiah revolted and formed an alliance with Egypt. The Babylonian super power swept into Judah and surrounded the city for approximately eighteen to thirty months. It was a terrible time for the people of Jerusalem.

Three years later the Babylonians broke through the walls (2 Kings 25:2–4; Jeremiah 39:2, 52:7; Ezekiel 33:21, 40:1). Zedekiah's sons were all killed and he was blinded and taken away as a prisoner.

Jerusalem was plundered and destroyed (2 Kgs 25:9–19; 2 Chr 36:18–19; Jer 52:12–25). Nothing was left standing, including the defensive walls that had once given the people a sense of security and identity.

Most people were taken away as slaves to serve in Babylon. Only a few people were allowed to stay and care for the land.

Fifty seven years later in 539 B.C. the Persian King, King Cyrus the Great defeated the Babylonian empire. The Jews were allowed little by little to return to Jerusalem. A new temple began to be built two years later in 537 B.C.

We start our story 64 years later in 445 B.C. with a new Persian King in charge called Artaxerxes and a full 141 years after the destruction of Jerusalem.

Characters:

Let me introduce some of the characters. Most of them go completely unnamed yet without them the rebuild of Jerusalem would not have happened.

People of Jerusalem: Most of the people would have been those who had returned from the exile in Babylon. They would not have known what Jerusalem was like prior to the destruction. They were a people rebuilding their personal identity.

Nehemiah: A Jew who served wine to the King of Persia. Nehemiah was the leader of the rebuild keeping the compelling vision of what was possible before the community. He was the leader that stood next to them. He wasn't aloof to their needs but had compassion for the community's rebuild.

King Artaxerxes I of Persia and his Queen; The reigning super power of the region. The capital was the city of Sush now called Shush in the country of Iran.

Sanballat, Tobiah, Geshem, the Arabians, the Ammonites, and the Ashdodites; The chief opponents of Nehemiah. They were leaders and local officials to the area.

1 Questions need to be asked

*The words of Nehemiah the son of Hacaliah. Now in the
month Chislev, in the twentieth year, as I was in Shushan
the palace, Hanani, one of my brothers, came, he and certain
men out of Judah; and I asked them concerning the Jews who
had escaped, who were left of the captivity, and concerning
Jerusalem. Nehemiah 1:1, 2*

It was the way they asked the question that really got me.
When I said 'I'm ok' to the usual 'How are you?'
introduction, they came back with 'No, how are you
really, we want to know'. This was one of those awkward
moments where I wanted to either carry on and play the
bluffing avoidance games and hope they don't pursue or
you step into the risk of being vulnerable.

Questions have a habit of opening up opportunities for
change. In fact, at the genesis of any change, will be
someone prepared to ask a question.

Is this the best that it can be? Can we improve? How can
I help? What needs to be done?

Many people want to avoid having questions asked of
them. Are you one of them?

Right at the commencement of our recovery journey
Nehemiah comes with a question.

How are the people of Jerusalem? We'll find out the
answer in the next chapter, but let's linger a moment with
this question.

It was a question that had a gentle curiosity to it. Nehemiah, as we will see later, was a man whose heart was for the welfare of others.

Questions need to be asked, but it's the way they are asked that will affect the outcome. Questions that lead to further gentle questions can empower a person to know that they are not alone.

Not every question needs an answer; it just needs to be asked.

Quote to consider

Most people go through their entire lives never speaking words to another human being that come out of what is deepest in them, and most people never hear words that reach all the way into that deep place we call the soul…

We almost never hear words that stir life within us, that pour hope into those empty spaces deep inside filled only with fear and frustration.

We rarely hear words that draw our soul into the soul of another human being and, together, into God. Dr Larry Crabb[1]

Question to answer
What are the qualities of a good question?

---

[1] Larry Crabb, Shattered Dreams: God's Unexpected Pathway to Joy

A rock to build with

A journey always begins with a question.

2 Embrace the truth

They said to me, "The remnant who are left of the captivity there in the province are in great affliction and reproach. The wall of Jerusalem also is broken down, and its gates are burned with fire." When I heard these words, **I sat down and wept, and mourned certain days; and I fasted and prayed** *before the God of heaven, Nehemiah 1:3,4*

Unexpected news can take us to places we aren't prepared for. When the diagnosis of cancer was given we know there is a hard road ahead. In that state of shock we console each other, we share our love and we grow strong in our shared weakness.

Let's not sugarcoat hard times. Life can hand us moments that call us to grieve. Actually, we must mourn. If we don't then how will we know the comfort and deep connection of God?

Nehemiah asked the question and got soul-destroying honest truth: 'Shame, great affliction, appalling conditions, wall is rubble, gates are cinders'

The people and the city were in a catastrophic mess. Survival was the daily challenge. Glorious Jerusalem was a ground down mess.

Words have a power that can cut to the very core of our hope.

But Nehemiah, whose name means 'Jehovah Comforts', went to Jehovah for comfort.

Sometimes the only thing we can and must do when hit by a freight train of emotions is to fall on the ground, weep, fast, and mourn. Out of that place of rawness, a groan rumbles into a prayer.

When the heart hits the basement, acknowledge it. Don't ignore the pain. It's there, real and it has a purpose.

Quote to consider
When we're looking for compassion, we need someone who is deeply rooted, able to bend, and, most of all, we need someone who embraces us for our strengths and struggles. Brene Brown[2]

Question to answer
Do you fear people's stories? Why?

A rock to build with
Embracing the rawness of pain invites a total dependence on God.

---

[2] Brene Brown. The Gifts of Imperfection

3 Deep connection grows heartfelt prayer

"I beg you, Yahweh, the God of heaven, the great and awesome God, who keeps covenant and loving kindness with those who love him and keep his commandments: Let your ear now be attentive, and your eyes open, that you may listen to the prayer of your servant, which I pray before you at this time, day and night, for the children of Israel your servants while I confess the sins of the children of Israel, which we have sinned against you. Yes, I and my father's house have sinned. We have dealt very corruptly against you, and have not kept the commandments, nor the statutes, nor the ordinances, which you commanded your servant Moses.
Nehemiah 1:5-7

The young man couldn't quite get his words together to explain his actions. He had invited me along to a disciplinary meeting with his boss. He had been caught speeding a few times by the police and now his delivery job was at risk.

The employer liked the young guy, so he was open to hearing how we could resolve the situation. I explained everything my family and I were going to do to help.

The employer was happy I had come and together we worked on a plan to curb the speeding problem.

The word 'intercede' means to act on behalf of someone else, to plead the case, to bridge the gap. Nehemiah comes before God and expresses his grief and need for the people of Jerusalem.

But he also goes one step further. He owns it himself. Sure, the destruction and humiliation of the people happened one hundred and forty years ago, but Nehemiah comes as one who is just like those who abandoned God's ways all those years ago.

There is a need in all of us for someone who at a deep level gets what we are going through. Someone who acknowledges their own flawed humanity and prays out of that.

Nehemiah, in a sense, embodied the people in pain.

The danger, if we take it too far, is that we take personal responsibility for others' choices. Nehemiah wasn't doing this, instead he was interceding on behalf of the people and including himself.

When we connect deeply with others we also see ourselves and from this place we can pray in honesty.

Quote to consider
Compassion means entering the suffering of another in order to lead the way out. Rosaria Champagne Butterfield[3]

Question for today
What is it like when someone who advocates or

---

[3] Rosaria Champagne Butterfield, The Secret Thoughts of an Unlikely Convert: An English Professor's Journey Into Christian Faith

intercedes on your behalf has a deep association with your struggle?

A rock to build with

A 'and next to them' person who will associate with your struggle.

4 The ancient of days

"Remember, I beg you, the word that you commanded your servant Moses, saying, 'If you trespass, I will scatter you abroad among the peoples; but if you return to me, and keep my commandments and do them, though your outcasts were in the uttermost part of the heavens, yet will I gather them from there, and will bring them to the place that I have chosen, to cause my name to dwell there.' Nehemiah 1:8,9

As I sat next to the groom on his wedding day I asked him how he was feeling. He said that he was only there because she got pregnant. Vows were made. Commitments and hopes expressed and I prayed that it would last.

All of us let people down in various ways. We don't always do what we say we will do. No one is 100% trustworthy.

Yet if we are going to build a strong life we need something or someone who is 100% reliable, trustworthy and is totally committed to our wellbeing.

Nehemiah comes to the ancient of days (Daniel 7:9) and advocates on the basis of vows made by God. We can do the same.

The 12 steps of Alcoholics Anonymous takes the struggler to the 'and next to them' relationship with God.

> *Step 2. Came to believe that a Power greater than ourselves could restore us to sanity.*
> *Step 3. Made a decision to turn our will and our lives over to the care of God as we understood God*

We are never alone in the rebuild. God is eternally committed to our recovery.

A power greater than our self is permanently right next to you.

Quote to consider
Spirituality is recognizing and celebrating that we are all inextricably connected to each other by a power greater than all of us, and that our connection to that power and to one another is grounded in love and compassion. Brene Brown[4]

Question to answer
What gets stirred up inside you, knowing that there is a 'power greater than yourself' ready to help?

A rock to build with
The 'ancient of days' is with us and is committed to our wellbeing.

---

[4] Brene Brown. The Gifts of Imperfection

5. Let's just focus on today

"Now these are your servants and your people, whom you have redeemed by your great power, and by your strong hand. Lord, I beg you, let your ear be attentive now to the prayer of your servant, and to the prayer of your servants, who delight to fear your name; and please prosper your servant today, and grant him mercy in the sight of this man." Nehemiah 1:10,11

Does your mind flit from thinking about the past to thinking about the future with momentary stop overs of being in the present?

Just to let you know, this is normal but not helpful. In fact when we focus too much on what has happened in the past we can become depressed. Focus on the future and we can become anxious.

The mind has a velcro like tendency to grip on to negative experiences and slippery teflon to the positive. It's part of a survival strategy developed to prepare us for the worst, but it's not a mindset that will lead to prosperity in heart and mind.

Nehemiah focused his prayer on the day ahead. He had a plan developing in his mind to seek the help of his employer the King. We will soon find that it was four months before he was able to lay out his plan to the King.

I wonder how many times Nehemiah's mind flitted between the experiences of the past and the 'what if' fears of future. Between what has happened and what could happen. How many times did he need to ground himself back into the present of today.

In addiction recovery, there is a focus of 'just for today'.

> *Just for today, I will try to live through this day only, and not tackle my whole life problem at once.*

Nehemiah prays for the prosperity of the day he was in. He prays for a prosperity of relationships that are next to him.

Live for today, just today.

Quote to consider
If you are depressed you are living in the past.
If you are anxious you are living in the future.
If you are at peace you are living in the present.
Lao Tzu

Question to answer
What struggles would be easier faced if you adopted a context of 'Just for this day'?

A rock to build with
God is with me in this day.

6. Right person, right place, right time and that time is now

Now I was cupbearer to the king. Nehemiah 1:11

One of my favourite Bible stories, one that gives me courage every day, is a short story of a wise but poor man.

The small city he lived in was under siege. He had some wisdom that he shared and it actually saved the city. He was in the right place at the right time, and dared to step up and offer some help.

After he had saved the city, he was forgotten about. No one knows his name, and that's okay. He did what was required, and that was enough. You can read the story in Ecclesiastes 9:14,15.

We also are in a place and a moment of time where we can be used of God for great things.

Seven words end the first chapter that can be easily overlooked; a time, a role, and a place of influence.

A cup-bearer was one that checked all the food and drink given at the King's table. If the King was suspicious that poison was in the Pinot Noir, then Nehemiah would have been the one to drink it first.

It was this level of trust and closeness to the King that gave Nehemiah such a unique God-orchestrated opportunity.

Nehemiah was the right person in the right place at the right time. God had positioned Nehemiah as a 'next to them' person to the most powerful person in the land.

Wherever you are right now is the place where you can serve.

Quote to consider
We must remember throughout our lives that in God's sight there are no little people and no little places. Only one thing is important: to be consecrated [dedicated] persons in God's place for us, at each moment. Francis Schaeffer[5]

Questions to answer
Where are you in the 'here and now' and what roles do you have? In what ways could you be the person for such a time as this?

A rock to build with
In God's sight there are no little people and no little places.

---

[5] Francis A. Schaeffer, No Little People (Wheaton, Ill.: Crossway, 2003)

7. Pre-prayed to pray

*In the month of Nisan, in the twentieth year of King
Artaxerxes, when wine was served him, I carried the wine
and gave it to the king. Now, I had never been sad in his
presence before.*

*So the king said to me, "Why is your face sad, since you are
not sick? This can only be sadness of the heart." Then I was
very much afraid.*

*I said to the king, "May the king live forever! Why should
my face not be sad, when the city, the place of my ancestors'
graves, lies waste, and its gates have been destroyed by fire?"*

*Then the king said to me, "What do you request?" So I
prayed to the God of heaven. Nehemiah 2:1-4*

'Are we there yet?' This was the annoying question
repeated countless times on our holiday journey. The kids
were tired of the drive and wanted it to be over. It was
taking longer than they had child-like patience for.

It only takes a second to turn the page from Nehemiah
chapter 1 to chapter 2 so it feels like Nehemiah prayed
and the next day he was in front of the King serving wine.

We like things to happen that quickly, don't we? Yet, with
the dates given, we discover that four months had passed
- four months of Nehemiah waiting and pre-praying his
plan for when the time was right. God was at work in
Nehemiah, but also he was at work in his employer - the
King.

Who was this King? Artaxerxes was the fifth King of Persia reigning from 465 BC to 424 BC. He was the most powerful man in the region. Like most kings, there was always someone wanting to take him down. His father had been killed by his bodyguard, so Artaxerxes had to have trusted servants close to him.

For someone as powerful as the King you weren't allowed just to go and ask for some help or advice. The King had to engage in the conversation first. An invitation needed to given. The King asked, and Nehemiah prayed.

When we pray, a battle ensues. This is a battle of the heart to do things our own way or to wait and allow God's hand to change the courses of the heart.

> *The king's heart is in Yahweh's hand like the watercourses.*
> *He turns it wherever he desires. Proverbs 21:1*

When we pray as Nehemiah did, something good happens in our heart. There is a connection, a power is released and the world starts to change.

Quote to consider
Prayers are tools not for doing or getting, but for being and becoming. Eugene Peterson[6]

---

[6] Eugene H. Peterson. Answering God: The Psalms as Tools for Prayer

Question to answer
What are you like at simply praying and waiting?

A rock to build with
When that moment of opportunity comes - pray.

8. We need a champion

Then I said to the king, "If it pleases the king, and if your servant has found favor with you, I ask that you send me to Judah, to the city of my ancestors' graves, so that I may rebuild it."

The king said to me (the queen also was sitting beside him), "How long will you be gone, and when will you return?" So it pleased the king to send me, and I set him a date.

Then I said to the king, "If it pleases the king, let letters be given me to the governors of the province Beyond the River, that they may grant me passage until I arrive in Judah; and a letter to Asaph, the keeper of the king's forest, directing him to give me timber to make beams for the gates of the temple fortress, and for the wall of the city, and for the house that I shall occupy."

And the king granted me what I asked, for the gracious hand of my God was upon me. Then I came to the governors beyond the River, and gave them the king's letters. Now the king had sent with me captains of the army and horsemen. Nehemiah 2:5-9

I was only a young man, maybe sixteen, when I went to the local farmers store and took an item off the shelf to the counter. I told them to put it on my father's account.

I felt ten feet tall. My father had given me the approval to go and do so. He approved of me, therefore others had to also.

Nehemiah's task was huge. It was something he could not do by himself, so he prayed. In fact, he prayed for four months. He and God were up to something good so that when the door opened to include others, Nehemiah grabbed it with prayer-filled hands.

We need champions - people with resources, respect or influence that we don't have; people who will champion our cause.

The momentum of change began to rumble into action all because God's gracious championing hand was on him.

Do you have a champion? Is there someone who will add resilience to you when things get tough? Are you a champion for someone else?

Quote to consider
If I am not for myself, who will be for me? But if I am only for myself, who am I? If not now, when? Hillel[7]

Questions to answer
How can you be a champion for someone else? What would it practically look like?

A rock to build with
We need people alongside us who will champion our cause.

---

[7] Hillel. Ethics of the Fathers, 1:14

9. Unsettling the settled stirs it up

*When Sanballat the Horonite, and Tobiah the servant, the Ammonite, heard of it, it grieved them exceedingly, because a man had come to seek the welfare of the children of Israel.
Nehemiah 2:10*

I was giving support to a young man in his early twenties who had schizophrenia. His mother, aged in her sixties, managed his finances for him. When I tried to support his desire to set up his own bank account and to learn about personal finance, he and I met stiff opposition from the mother.

She feared losing control. Eventually, she withdrew him from the agency I was working for, and he went home.

Nehemiah was on his way to Jerusalem. Everything was going to plan but not everyone liked the plan. Some of those living in and near Jerusalem had been doing quite well from broken people, but now with Nehemiah and his champions, that all looked under threat.

Empowerment of the individual often leads to friction with others. A move to rebuild may be met with a move to tear down.

When we are rebuilding, there will be voices of opposition. They may be the thoughts and feelings swirling around in our mind, but they may well come from people - some that are close to us. They want to keep us in a box that they feel safe with.

For every push forward in life there will be a push back; an energy that will want you to stay the same or retreat further.

From here on in, Nehemiah faced struggle after struggle with a few victories along the way.

Quote to consider
The moment our hearts begin to feel any level of freedom and goodness, the kingdom of darkness is not going to relent in its dark, pernicious, relentless, violent commitment to do harm to the glory of God and anyone who bears anything of the mark of God's glory. The moment your life begins to move, you will face the hatred of the kingdom of darkness, and often something of the envy of friends, family who do not wish your change to have any kind of influence on their lives. Dan Allender[8]

Questions to answer
What voices in yourself and from others, oppose the needed change? Why?

A rock to build with
There will always be a push back to your pushing forward.

----

[8] Dan Allender. Podcast - Healing the Wounded Heart, Part One, February 13, 2016

10. There is always more underneath

So I came to Jerusalem, and was there three days. I arose in the night, I and some few men with me; neither told I any man what my God put into my heart to do for Jerusalem; neither was there any animal with me, except the animal that I rode on. I went out by night by the valley gate, even toward the jackal's well, and to the dung gate, and viewed the walls of Jerusalem, which were broken down, and its gates were consumed with fire. Then I went on to the spring gate and to the king's pool: but there was no place for the animal that was under me to pass. Then went I up in the night by the brook, and viewed the wall; and I turned back, and entered by the valley gate, and so returned. The rulers didn't know where I went, or what I did; neither had I as yet told it to the Jews, nor to the priests, nor to the nobles, nor to the rulers, nor to the rest who did the work. Nehemiah 2:11-16

On first appearances, everything looked great until you went underneath. The old house had that lovely country cottage feel about it, but as time went on discoveries were made of rotting walls, leaking pipes and drains not working.

There was always going to be more underneath than what was first realized.

Nehemiah arrived in Jerusalem, and after a few days of rest he sneaked out at night for a quick inspection.

There is always more underneath in us too. We like to make good appearances, to impress and convince others that we are OK. Underneath though, we all have a pile of rubble that can be built into something of both purpose and beauty.

We want to be known and to have others join us in our journey, yet we are also afraid of what they might do if they truly went below the surface.

Nehemiah's Jerusalem was exposed. Anyone could come and rampage through its soul and take what they wanted, leaving them even more desolate. It took a brave and compassionate man to explore the rubble; to be next to them, and own it for themselves.

Building a life out of rubble requires guts and a willingness just to take that next step, whatever that might be.

There will be places that seem impassable, where we see that there is no other way forward but through the raw, painful honesty of the soul. 'This is me, and this is how it is.'

God knows everything about it and promises to build with us.

Quote to consider
Curiosity will not discover anything that grace cannot handle. Larry Crabb

Question to answer
Are you afraid to go deep and find out what is hidden under the surface rubble? Why?

A rock to build with
There is always more underneath, and God knows it all.

11. We rebuild together

Then I said to them, "You see the evil case that we are in, how Jerusalem lies waste, and its gates are burned with fire. Come, let us build up the wall of Jerusalem, that we won't be disgraced." Nehemiah 2:17

When I said to them that I would go with them to the doctor a huge sense of relief washed over them. I also said that I would do whatever I could, to help them find others who would walk alongside them too.

Friends, nurses, therapists, family members, all took a level of ownership of the problem.

Nehemiah could have said it was their problem to solve. He could have told them what they should do. He could have sat back and given out 'good' advice. He could have just said 'Let's pray about that'. He could have done nothing and gone home.

Instead, Nehemiah owned the problem as his own. He committed himself to going deep. This cemented the loyalty of the people to the vision he was going to give.

Nehemiah stepped forward with courage, explored the rubble and said 'I am with you in this mess, let's rebuild together. I can do what I can do; you will do what you can do and together we will shift rubble.'

That is the 'and next to them' message of this book.

We were never meant to be alone in our build. We build together.

So in prayer, and with gentle curiosity, we invite a taste of knowing others. In this place of knowing, we carry this burden to God asking what it is that we are called to do.

Quote to consider
Do for one what you wish you could do for everyone.
Andy Stanley[9]

Question to answer
What happens in the heart when you experience the joining of someone on your journey?

A rock to build with
Recovery is a journey done with others.

---

[9] Andy Stanley. Sermon Northpoint Church

12. The Compelling Vision

*I told them of the hand of my God which was good on me, as
also of the king's words that he had spoken to me.
They said, "Let's rise up and build." So they strengthened
their hands for the good work. Nehemiah 2:18*

One of the greatest speeches ever made was the 'I have a
dream' speech from Martin Luther King. He calls the
listener to look beyond the present struggle to a time
where things will be different. He gives a vision that the
listener is compelled to go after.

If we want to grow confidence in others, tell a great story.

Nehemiah had grown in confidence and was now ready
for action. He could relate how God had been at work to
bring him to this point and about the support of the king.
But he could not do it by himself. Would they commit?
Would they come together for the project? Decisions
would have to be made.

At times I have written vision letters for people. In these
letters, I write what I believe God is up to in their lives
and who they might become. I give them a tangible
written gift of what I believe God is doing. The gift is a
belief in a better future and that I believe in them.

Often we get mired down in the mud of our present
situation. The mud then turns to concrete and our minds
lock us in. A compelling vision is one that calls us to
make the small millimetre steps of challenge and change.

I don't believe this sense of vision can be generated from
within ourselves. This is why we need others. Most likely

these others are those who have been there, done that and can hold a lamp of hope out for us. A beam of light is cast out onto a path that we can take together.

This is what Nehemiah did for those broken people.

Quote to consider
The compelling vision is . . . maybe, because of our conversations, we can want God more than we want any lesser blessing. Larry Crabb[10]

Question to answer
How do we discover a compelling vision for others?

A rock to build with
A vision of how things could be different compels us to move forward.

---

[10] Soulcare foundations 201: Lesson 1

13. They don't get to choose the music

But when Sanballat the Horonite, and Tobiah the servant, the Ammonite, and Geshem the Arabian, heard it, they ridiculed us, and despised us, and said, "What is this thing that you are doing? Will you rebel against the king?"

Then answered I them, and said to them, "The God of heaven will prosper us. Therefore we, his servants, will arise and build; but you have no portion, nor right, nor memorial, in Jerusalem." Nehemiah 2:19-20

'You can't do that! You're going to fail and then what will others think.'

Don't you just get frustrated when others come along and shoot your ideas down? You have a compelling vision, a dream that things could be different, then it's subjected to harsh critical abuse.

Nehemiah and the people chose to step out onto the wobbly rubble. Immediately, stones were thrown at the plans; stones of mockery and ridicule, but Nehemiah was ready.

Nehemiah knew these influences. He had probably already faced them back when he was serving wine to the king, but he had learnt a little secret. He had learnt to acknowledge them and to put them in their place, in the back seat.

Liz Gilbert writes a letter to fear.

Dearest fear, you're allowed to have a seat, and you're allowed to have a voice, but you are not allowed to have a vote.

You're not allowed to touch the road maps; you're not allowed to suggest detours; you're not allowed to fiddle with the temperature.

Dude, you're not even allowed to touch the radio.

But above all else, my dear old familiar friend, you are absolutely forbidden to drive.[11]

In the same way, Nehemiah acknowledged those voices of ridicule but confined them to the back of the bus. God is with us, and God will be in our front seat. The voices of mockery are not going to have any reward for this journey.

As we continue with Nehemiah, we will continue to hear those voices from the back seat clambering to get in the front.

Nehemiah wouldn't let them.

Quote to consider
People who say it cannot be done should not interrupt those who are doing it. George Bernard Shaw

---

[11] Elizabeth Gilbert, Big Magic: Creative Living Beyond Fear

Question to answer
What inner voices do you need to acknowledge and put in the back seat?

A rock to build with
The voices of opposition will always be there but we don't have to listen to them.

14. Be strong and do the work

Then Eliashib the high priest rose up with his brothers the priests, and they built the sheep gate; they sanctified it, and set up its doors; even to the tower of Hammeah they sanctified it, to the tower of Hananel. Nehemiah 3:1

The old saying is true. You can lead a horse to water, but you can't make it drink. It's also true that you can take the water to the horse, put the water in a china cup and sprinkle rose petals over and it still won't drink.

In my years as a pastor - chaplain - mental health worker, I found that the ones who made progress and saw recovery were the ones who did the work. They didn't sit around smoking all day, regaling the old days or just accepting their lot. They were the ones who made the effort to change.

The words had been said, inspections made and commitments voiced. But would the people of Jerusalem start? Would they put their hands to the work?

Nehemiah 3 begins with the word 'Then', and it speaks to the deliberate choice to start.

Who starts? The leaders start. The high priest and his family show the way.

Seriously, we all want someone else to do the work. But it's in doing the work that we find the gold of transformation, recovery and hope.

Don't be a P.L.O.M. (Poor Little Old Me), instead 'Be strong and do the work'. 1 Chronicles 28:9-10

Quote to consider
It is not the critic who counts;
not the man who points out how the strong man
stumbles,
or where the doer of deeds could have done them better.
The credit belongs to the man who is actually in the
arena,
whose face is marred by dust and sweat and blood;
who strives valiantly; who errs, who comes short again
and again,
because there is no effort without error and shortcoming;
but who does actually strive to do the deeds;
who knows great enthusiasms, the great devotions;
who spends himself in a worthy cause;
who at the best knows in the end the triumph of high
achievement,
and who at the worst, if he fails, at least fails while daring
greatly,
so that his place shall never be with those cold and timid
souls who neither know victory nor defeat.
Theodore Roosevelt

Question to answer
Where do we need to 'Be strong and do the work'?

A rock to build with
There is always a choice to do the work or not.

15. One plus one doesn't equal two

*Next to him built the men of Jericho. Next to them built
Zaccur the son of Imri. Nehemiah 3:1, 2*

My nephew has one of those little drone aircraft. With it,
he can fly high above our house and send pictures down
to us.

If we were to fly a little drone above the rebuilding of the
Jerusalem wall, we would find groups of people, all
working next to each other. The phrase 'and next to
them' is mentioned 26 times in Nehemiah 3.

A ring of workers encompass the fragile soul, all with a
compelling vision that life can and will be different. All of
them are flawed in various ways, but all are open to be
used to create.

Recovery, rebuilding, and indeed life, is a 'next to them'
project.

I think of the people I have supported, and also of
myself, who having discovered a few safe others then a
momentum is found. Words jump in the heart 'So you
too!'

One plus one no longer equals two, but in the
relationship there is a multiplication of momentum. I can
imagine how on that ancient construction site there
would have been a rhythm, perhaps a song, and tools
shared. Common purpose, language, and focus.

Life grows and flourishes when we have others around us
on a similar journey. Those next to us have similar

bumps, bruises, scars and calluses. It's in isolation and individualism that we can so easily lose our way.

Are we open to hearing the voices of others who are on a similar journey?

Quote to consider
Friendship is born at that moment when one person says to another: "What! You too? I thought I was the only one." C. S. Lewis[12]

Question to answer
What stops us from being in close 'and next to them' relationships?

A rock to build with
You're not the only one.

---

[12] C.S. Lewis, The Four Loves

16. Get your hands dirty!

Next to them, the Tekoites made repairs; but their nobles didn't put their necks to the work of their lord. Nehemiah 3:5

As a child, I was read the story of the Little Red Hen. The story describes a little hen asking all her barnyard friends to help with the various activities of growing a crop of wheat right through to the baking of the bread.

When asking for help to sow the seed, weed the garden, harvest the crop etc. the horse, cow, sheep all said 'Oh, No not I.' That was until the smell of freshly baked bread wafted across the barnyard, and all offered to help Little Red Hen to eat the bread, to which she declined their generosity.

In Nehemiah's story, we have a group of 'nobles' who refused to be part of the 'next to them' team. They are now forever known as being snobs, and as those who refused the call to rebuild.

There are some who don't want to do the work - in fact, any work at all! They want to savour the feast without serving in the kitchen.

This act of rebuilding, recovery, and restoration is something we are all invited to be part of.

It's not nice, predictable and controlled work. It's quite frankly, mysterious and at times damned scary. We are not in control, but there is one who knows every speck of dirt and dust and has a plan for the restoration.

Rebuild. Are you part of it? Or are you too proud to get your hands dirty?

Quote to consider
Christianity did not come in order to develop the heroic virtues in the individual but rather to remove self-centeredness and establish love. Soren Kierkegaard

Question to answer
What character qualities do those that do the unglamourous 'next to them' work name?

A rock to build with
The reward is for those who do the work.

17. I say 'Resurrection' to the mocker

But when Sanballat heard that we were building the wall, he was angry, and took great indignation, and mocked the Jews. He spoke before his brothers and the army of Samaria, and said, "What are these feeble Jews doing? Will they fortify themselves? Will they sacrifice? Will they finish in a day? Will they revive the stones out of the heaps of rubbish, since they are burned?" Now Tobiah the Ammonite was by him, and he said, "What they are building, if a fox climbed up it, he would break down their stone wall." Nehemiah 4:1-3

I don't think I could ever be a politician. I look at what politicians have to put up with and know I couldn't handle it. There is adulation one day, then a knife in the back the next.

There are all those negative voices. People, wanting to tear you down, are ready to do anything to achieve your destruction.

The build was on, and the people were breaking free. Stone upon stone was being laid, and progress was being made. But not everyone was happy. Not everyone was part of the build. Some chose to throw the stones rather than to build with them. Words were spoken to try and undermine the rebuild.

'Will they revive the stones out of the heaps of rubbish, since they are burned?'

Burnt stones don't make strong walls - they are brittle. But God is reviving those stones that others dismiss.

The word that jumps out at me with startling thunderous applause is 'RESURRECTION'.

The act of new life is springing up out of that which was dead.

Our rebuild will require an element of resurrection presence. The audacity of God to be able to bring something that was completely dead back to life, and then for that life to become something more glorious than before, shouts hope to me.

In every seemingly impossible situation, we need to shout 'RESURRECTION'.

The addiction, the trauma, the violence all need the power of resurrection to turn stones back to life from those heaps of rubble—burnt as they are.

In the face of mockers, I shout 'Resurrection!'

Quote to consider
Shame drives two tapes. 'You're never good enough' and 'Who do you think you are' Brene Brown[13]

Question to answer
What voices mock you and your rebuild?

A rock to build with
To the voices that would kill progress we shout 'Resurrection!'

---

[13] Brene Brown. Ted Talk Listening to Shame

18. God can handle your raw anger

"Hear, our God; for we are despised; and turn back their reproach on their own head, give them up for a plunder in a land of captivity; don't cover their iniquity, and don't let their sin be blotted out from before you; for they have insulted the builders." Nehemiah 4:4, 5

I'm glad that some of the prayers I have prayed, God didn't follow through on. I had let all the rawness of my pain just flow. I've not had many people in my life where I could do this with and not receive some form of judgement, band-aid advice or rejection and abandonment.

Wouldn't it be good to have a few safe friends where you could just spill your guts, say it like it is and let it all out? It would be like a big pressure tank emptying itself out.

Instead we hold it all in, keep up appearances, and not let our true self be seen.

Nehemiah had heard the mocking, and something snapped inside him. He prayed his raw feelings out. He didn't repress them or hold them back. He let God know what he wants God to do.

God welcomed Nehemiah's rawness and welcomes ours also.

It's OK to be angry, and seriously I think we could get more angry, about a lot of things, and it would help.

Anger is an emotion, just as much as joy is. It is God-given and is part of the character of God. It's what we do with our anger that matters. Do we bottle it up in an internalised pressure tank or let it flow out before God.

Quote to consider
All great spirituality is about what we do with our pain. Richard Rohr[14]

Question to answer
What do you do with your anger? How can you safely vent the pressure inside?

A rock to build with
Emotions are normal. It's what we do with them that matters.

---

[14] Richard Rohr, Adam's Return: The Five Promises of Male Initiation

19. Having a mind to work

So we built the wall; and all the wall was joined together to half its height: for the people had a mind to work. Nehemiah 4:6

He always struck me as someone who focused on pushing against the odds. Just because he had a diagnosis of schizophrenia, he was not going to let this be a defining label over his life. He had a mind to do the work. He read about his illness, sought out support to help him achieve his goals and never took a backward step into the mire of accepting that this was his lot in life.

Through his positive attitude and willingness to give things a try, he was a positive role model to those who were standing next to him.

Nehemiah's community of wall-builders were halfway there because they had a mind to do the work. The will and the heart found an energy and a purpose. There was a passionate determination to build the wall. It wasn't a job; it was a burning desire to accomplish something great.

In recovery, we can come to a point where we think we have made it; that we have finished and have won the battle. We think that we no longer need to do the work. In reality we are only halfway there and there is always more to do.

Does this cause you some level of dismay? It will do if we shift all the problems and pains of yesterday on to the unknown of tomorrow. When we do this, the problems always seem to grow.

Instead, focus on today. Nehemiah's builders could not build the wall of tomorrow without shifting the stones of today. Focus on this moment and this day, so you can nourish the mind that is doing the work.

Do you have a 'mind to work'?

Quote to consider
A vision we give to others of who and what they could become has power when it echoes what the Spirit has already spoken into their souls. Larry Crabb[15]

Question to answer
What encourages your mind to do the work?

A rock to build with
Halfway there? Keep going.

---

[15] Larry Crabb. Connecting: Healing Ourselves and Our Relationships

20. Power dynamics that threaten

But when Sanballat, Tobiah, the Arabians, the Ammonites, and the Ashdodites heard that the repairing of the walls of Jerusalem went forward, and that the breaches began to be filled, then they were very angry; and they conspired all of them together to come and fight against Jerusalem, and to cause confusion therein. But we made our prayer to our God, and set a watch against them day and night, because of them. Nehemiah 4:7-9

A friend recently asked, 'Do you know what the 'Golden Rule' is?' He then went on to say that, 'He who has the gold makes the rules'. If you live under the motto, 'If mama ain't happy, then nobody is happy' then mama is the one who holds the power.

Power dynamics, or how power plays itself out in the relationships we have, can get thoroughly upended when we start to change. As we get stronger in our belief about ourselves, others may well feel threatened. When we aren't so easily walked over, it means that others have to make changes themselves.

Halfway there and the wall was taking shape and casting a shadow on its opposers. Power dynamics were changing, so plans were made to undermine the confidence of the builders.

Nehemiah reported that the people prayed and posted a guard. They reinforced the relationship strength they had; more of God and more of each other.

There is strength with numbers. Confidence, courage and hope grow when we have others alongside us praying and keeping guard.

When you feel like your change is being threatened, call out to the guards - those 'and next to them' stalwarts. Have them bolster your heart.

Quote to consider
Beneath what our culture calls psychological disorder is a soul crying out for what only community can provide. Larry Crabb[16]

Question to answer
Who is standing beside you as 'guards', watching out for threats that would want to tear down the progress?

A rock to build with
Courage grows in community.

---

[16] Larry Crabb. Connecting: Healing Ourselves and Our Relationships

21. When Fatigue hits your heart

Judah said, "The strength of the bearers of burdens is fading, and there is much rubbish; so that we are not able to build the wall." Our adversaries said, "They shall not know, neither see, until we come in among them, and kill them, and cause the work to cease."

When the Jews who lived by them came, they said to us ten times from all places, "Wherever you turn, they will attack us." Therefore set I in the lowest parts of the space behind the wall, in the open places, I set the people after their families with their swords, their spears, and their bows. I looked, and rose up, and said to the nobles, and to the rulers, and to the rest of the people, "Don't be afraid of them! Remember the Lord, who is great and awesome, and fight for your brothers, your sons, and your daughters, your wives, and your houses." Nehemiah 4: 10-14

He got so tired of the battle and the seemingly endless struggle, that he wanted out. It was all becoming just too much for him to carry. Having battled his addiction for years it got the better of him, and when his whole world crashed in around him, he wanted to die.

Fatigue is the wearing down of the soul until there is but a thread of existence. We just want to stop and give up.

Those on the rebuilding project had hit the rubble wall of fatigue. Alongside the mountains of rubble to shift, there were threats and gossiping of failure swirling around them like pesky mosquitoes.

The builders weren't superheroes, they were people just like us.

Nehemiah did what he does best. He reinforced the 'and next to them' relationships. He refocused the weary eyes to look up and remember the character of God as being great and awesome; to not be afraid, but to fight for those closest to them - 'your brothers, your sons, and your daughters, your wives, and your houses.'

If we are so fatigued of soul that we want to give up, we must remember that everyone is fighting a huge battle, and we all need each other.

We build for the strengthening of each other, so we give gifts of encouragement, meagre as they may be, to each other.

Nehemiah gave heart to the people.

Quote to consider
The word encouragement has its root in the Latin word cor, which literally means "heart". So does the word courage. To have courage means to have heart. To encourage – to provide with or give courage – literally means to give others heart. Richard I, King of England from 1189 to 1199, was glorified for his courage.How was he called by the troubadours? Richard the Lion-Hearted. Kouzes Posner[17]

Question to answer
What are the qualities of a friend who knows how to speak life into a fatigued heart?

[17] Jim Kouzes and Barry Posner "Encouraging the Heart – A leader's guide to rewarding and recognizing others"

A rock to build with
Close relationships help when fatigue hits the heart.

22. Where you stare you'll steer

When our enemies heard that it was known to us, and God had brought their counsel to nothing, all of us returned to the wall, everyone to his work. Nehemiah 4:15

On regular occasions, I travel on a road that is outside of the area where I live. It's beautiful countryside and many of the roads are long and straight, but it's one of the most dangerous roads you can drive on. When I first started driving this road, I noticed signposts that I had not seen anywhere else.

One of them showed a motorbike with the rider looking slightly off to the left. Underneath were the words, 'Where you stare you'll steer'. The warning was about how the brain seems to take your body to where your eyes are looking. So at high speed, you can dangerously drift away from your intended direction.

Nehemiah and his team of his builders had plenty of distractions happening around them. It would have been so easy to have kept a gaze on the problems; to focus on failures and threats rather than the progress and the future.

According to Dr Rick Hanson, the brain is like 'Velcro for negative experiences, but Teflon for positive ones.'

Nehemiah keeps the focus on what is truly important - the Build. The builders could have velcroed the threats to their brains and ended up in the ditch. Instead, they returned to the build and to each person's place on that wall.

Life has many dangerous distractions. If we stare at them long enough, we will end up in the ditch. Return your mind to what is truly important.

Quote to consider
Since every destination starts as a thought, I focus on where I want to go. Paul Crawford

Question to answer
What are the little distractions that can cause us to drift off course?

A rock to build with
Where you stare you'll steer.

23 Don't let your guard down

From that time forth, half of my servants worked in the work, and half of them held the spears, the shields, and the bows, and the coats of mail; and the rulers were behind all the house of Judah. They all built the wall and those who bore burdens loaded themselves; everyone with one of his hands worked in the work, and with the other held his weapon; and the builders, everyone wore his sword at his side, and so built. Nehemiah 4:16-18

'You can always find an excuse to drink' were the profound words an alcoholic once told me. A rainy day, work, bad news, good news, all can be used as reasons to have a drink.

They had learnt the hard way that those reasons were liars they had set up in their thinking. To combat them they had set up guards - people they could talk to who would help them think through some better options. They had learnt to listen to themselves, take responsibility and choose healthier options.

Never let your guard down. The temptation is always there to sweep us away.

Progress was being made in the rebuild, but now it was with a keen awareness of the danger around them. While one hand laid a stone down, the other hand held a spear. Always on guard, always building. Everyone had a common purpose and vision of building the wall and a new identity.

It would have been tight work. The guards would have been alert, tense and watchful. They could not let their guard down for a moment. The one building would have been highly focused on getting the task done, because they would not have wanted to let the one guarding them down.

Both guard and builder owned the build together. 'And next to them' was a marriage of oneness for the benefit of all.

We need to be responsible for ourselves and the choices we make. However we need others to be around us who will watch out for threats; others who will call us out when we make lame excuses for poor behaviour.

Quote to consider
Groups tend to emphasize accountability when they don't know how to relate. Larry Crabb[18]

Question to answer
Who have you invited to be a watching guard next to your rebuild?

A rock to build with
Building partners watch out for places of potential failure.

---

[18] Larry Crabb. Connecting: Healing Ourselves and Our Relationships

24. There's strength in numbers

He who sounded the trumpet was by me. I said to the nobles, and to the rulers and to the rest of the people, "The work is great and large, and we are separated on the wall, one far from another. Wherever you hear the sound of the trumpet, rally there to us. Our God will fight for us."Nehemiah 4:19-20

There was a time in my life when I was struggling with my depression. I had seen a psychiatrist and went under the care of the local Mental Health team. Every day I would receive a call from someone on the team asking how my day was going. I made progress slowly and purposefully.

I remember those calls as having that 'and next to them' quality. Someone was in my corner. Someone who knew the fight at a professional level and could rally others to my assistance if needed. I also had friends who I could call at a moment's notice, and they would help too.

Each individual wall builder had a buddy, a team, a cohort of fellow builders that would rally to their aid at a moment's notice. The trumpet would sound, and strength in numbers would appear.

Isolation can lead to weakness and vulnerability. We pridefully think we can do this rebuild on our own, but we need others who can quickly come to bolster the flagging soul.

There is strength in numbers. A few others can rally a few more, and we get through the battle.

Quote to consider
Real encouragement occurs when words are spoken from a heart of love to another's recognized fear. Larry Crabb

Question to answer
What challenges do you face as you consider allowing others into the areas where you're vulnerable?

A rock to build with
We rebuild with others.

25. Don't take off your clothes

So we worked in the work: and half of them held the spears from the rising of the morning until the stars appeared. Likewise at the same time said I to the people, "Let everyone with his servant lodge within Jerusalem, that in the night they may be a guard to us, and may labor in the day." So neither I, nor my brothers, nor my servants, nor the men of the guard who followed me, none of us took off our clothes. Everyone took his weapon to the water. Nehemiah 4:21-23

Due to a food allergy, I have never been able to eat eggs or anything made with eggs. Many cakes, desserts, and meals I am not able to eat. This has been a hassle for me all my life and for those around me. At times I have ended up in a hospital when a little egg has slipped through my guard. One time it was when someone used a serving spoon in a dessert with egg in it then placed the spoon into a dessert with no egg. Cross-contamination landed me in a hospital within an hour.

I always have to be on my guard. This is part of who I am, and it's my personal responsibility to keep it that way.

Nehemiah, in this stage of the rebuild, never took his clothes off. Those with him never took their clothes off. What a smelly bunch of builders they would have been, but they were deadly serious about the threats. They never let their guard down, not for a moment.

When we take the threats we are up against seriously we realise that the slippery slope to destruction is but a footstep of relaxation away. We build guard-rails and warning signs as the clothes we always wear. We never let our guard down.

Quote to consider
Today, our very survival depends on our ability to stay awake, to adjust to new ideas, to remain vigilant and to face the challenge of change. Martin Luther King, Jr.

Question to answer
What does being vigilant look like for you?

A rock to build with
Be on your guard always.

26. A voice is found

*Then there arose a great cry of the people and of their wives
against their brothers the Jews. For there were that said,
"We, our sons and our daughters, are many. Let us get
grain, that we may eat and live." Some also there were that
said, "We are mortgaging our fields, and our vineyards, and
our houses. Let us get grain, because of the famine." There
were also some who said, "We have borrowed money for the
king's tribute using our fields and our vineyards as collateral.
Yet now our flesh is as the flesh of our brothers, our children
as their children. Behold, we bring into bondage our sons and
our daughters to be servants, and some of our daughters have
been brought into bondage. Neither is it in our power to help
it; for other men have our fields and our vineyards."
Nehemiah 5:1-5*

For years John had said nothing. He had watched and
tried to work out why this bully was treating him in such
a terrible way. He had been bullied as a child, so
whenever he saw this man flex his tongue he would
shrink away. But something was growing within him. A
courage and belief in himself that his opinions mattered
and that he had a right to be heard.

Choosing the right time and place, and with help from
others, he confronted the abuser. The bully was taken
aback at first and tried to dodge the probing questions.
He knew his days of tyranny were numbered.

John's self-belief grew. He discovered that he didn't have
to be a bully to confront the bully, but instead he used his
wisdom to undermine the shaky castle the bully lived in.

When a person's self-belief grows, and the child comes out of the shadows, a voice begins to be heard.

Many of the people in Jerusalem were under the mortgage (death grip in Latin) weight of their fellow Jews. They were selling their children into slavery just to survive. So while a wall was being built, a debt was crippling the soul. However with every stone laid, every foot of wall height gained, there was equally a growth in the self. The injustices were becoming more and more self-evident, and something needed to be said.

There is a time to say it like it is, to find your voice and speak the truth.

Quote to Consider
It's not about finding your voice, it's about giving yourself permission to use your voice. Kris Carr

Question to answer
What helps you to 'use your voice'?

A rock to build with
Expressing your reality is a step to changing your reality.

27. We all need 'Big People'

I was very angry when I heard their cry and these words. Then I consulted with myself, and contended with the nobles and the rulers, and said to them, "You exact usury, everyone of his brother." I held a great assembly against them. I said to them, "We, after our ability, have redeemed our brothers the Jews that were sold to the nations; and would you even sell your brothers, and should they be sold to us?" Then they held their peace, and found never a word. Also I said, "The thing that you do is not good. Ought you not to walk in the fear of our God, because of the reproach of the nations our enemies? I likewise, my brothers and my servants, lend them money and grain. Please let us stop this usury. Please restore to them, even today, their fields, their vineyards, their olive groves, and their houses, also the hundredth part of the money, and of the grain, the new wine, and the oil, that you are charging them."

Then they said, "We will restore them, and will require nothing of them; so will we do, even as you say."

Then I called the priests, and took an oath of them, that they would do according to this promise. Also I shook out my lap, and said, "So may God shake out every man from his house, and from his labor, that doesn't perform this promise; even thus be he shaken out, and emptied."

All the assembly said, "Amen," and praised Yahweh. The people did according to this promise. Nehemiah 5:6-13

I don't remember many of the tributes given about my father at his funeral, but this one stands out. A fellow church-goer recalled that in Church business meetings, that my father had a certain presence about him. You knew that he was there or not without looking to see if he was. He had wisdom and a gentle presence about him that strengthened hearts. He was a big person.

Nehemiah was a big person. He was someone who had a deep wisdom and would come alongside when needed.

Nehemiah stepped up to the injustices faced by the people and he advocates for their welfare. He didn't sit aloof from their needs. Instead, he embraced them as his own and confronted the abusers head on. The changes came swiftly.

We all, at times need big people to stand next to us, to offer us a strength that we cannot muster within ourselves. We all need someone to advocate on our behalf.

Quote to consider
Don't walk in front of me… I may not follow
Don't walk behind me… I may not lead
Walk beside me… just be my friend
Albert Camus

Question to answer
What are the qualities of a 'big person' for you?

A rock to build with
Strength is found in community.

28 She cleaned toilets too

Moreover from the time that I was appointed to be their governor in the land of Judah, from the twentieth year even to the two and thirtieth year of Artaxerxes the king, that is, twelve years, I and my brothers have not eaten the bread of the governor. But the former governors who were before me were supported by the people, and took bread and wine from them, besides forty shekels of silver; yes, even their servants ruled over the people: but I didn't do so, because of the fear of God. Yes, also I continued in the work of this wall, neither bought we any land: and all my servants were gathered there to the work. Moreover there were at my table, of the Jews and the rulers, one hundred fifty men, besides those who came to us from among the nations that were around us. Now that which was prepared for one day was one ox and six choice sheep; also fowls were prepared for me, and once in ten days store of all sorts of wine: yet for all this I didn't demand the bread of the governor, because the bondage was heavy on this people. Remember to me, my God, for good, all that I have done for this people. Nehemiah 5:14-19

When a well-dressed man came looking for Mother Teresa of Calcutta, he was told by the nuns that she was at the rear of the house cleaning the toilets. When he found her, she was indeed cleaning toilets. She assumed he was there to volunteer, so she gave him a toilet brush and demonstrated how to hold the brush correctly and to use as little water as possible. She then left him to it.

Nehemiah was one of us. He did not take advantage of his powerful role for personal advantage. Others beforehand had added burden upon burden until the bondage was heavy on the people.

Nehemiah lived in fear of God. However, this wasn't a worried state of fear of what God might do if he didn't obey. Fear never grows hope. This fear was a deep reverence for God, a desire to do things God would delight in.

There is no hierarchy of prestige among God's people. We are all made from dust and will return to dust once again. Jesus washed the dust off feet like yours and mine.

Those that will contribute the most to you will be the ones that know their dustiness.

Quote to consider
Prayer in action is love, love in action is service. Mother Teresa

Question to answer
As an act of service what would delight God's heart today?

A rock to build with
Quiet acts build great lives.

29. A great work

Now when it was reported to Sanballat and Tobiah, and to Geshem the Arabian, and to the rest of our enemies, that I had built the wall, and that there was no breach left therein; (though even to that time I had not set up the doors in the gates;) Sanballat and Geshem sent to me, saying, "Come, let us meet together in the villages in the plain of Ono." But they intended to harm me.

I sent messengers to them, saying, "I am doing a great work, so that I can't come down. Why should the work cease, while I leave it, and come down to you?" They sent to me four times after this sort; and I answered them the same way.

Then Sanballat sent his servant to me the same way the fifth time with an open letter in his hand, in which was written, "It is reported among the nations, and Gashmu says it, that you and the Jews intend to rebel. Because of that, you are building the wall. You would be their king, according to these words. You have also appointed prophets to preach of you at Jerusalem, saying, 'There is a king in Judah!' Now it will be reported to the king according to these words. Come now therefore, and let us take counsel together."

Then I sent to him, saying, "There are no such things done as you say, but you imagine them out of your own heart." For they all would have made us afraid, saying, "Their hands will be weakened from the work, that it not be done." But now, strengthen my hands.

I went to the house of Shemaiah the son of Delaiah the son of Mehetabel, who was shut in at his home; and he said, "Let us meet together in God's house, within the temple, and let us shut the doors of the temple; for they will come to kill you; yes, in the night will they come to kill you."

I said, "Should such a man as I flee? Who is there that, being such as I, would go into the temple to save his life? I will not go in." I discerned, and behold, God had not sent him; but he pronounced this prophecy against me. Tobiah and Sanballat had hired him. He hired so that I would be afraid, do so, and sin, and that they might have material for an evil report, that they might reproach me. "Remember, my God, Tobiah and Sanballat according to these their works, and also the prophetess Noadiah, and the rest of the prophets, that would have put me in fear." Nehemiah 6:1-14

So many times I am tempted to give up on writing. I wonder if what I am doing makes a difference, yet I keep on writing because I believe I am doing 'a great work'. I believe that my words do count and help people. Occasionally I get some feedback that puts a bit more fuel in the tank.

Nehemiah was nearing the end of the build. He could see the finishing line, and his enemies could too. So a plan was hatched to get him away from the project; to distract him.

The Valley of Ono was a pleasant area where Nehemiah could have kicked back, revelled in his achievements and then lost momentum. It was also a place where he may well have been killed.

However, he kept his focus on that next stone to be put on the wall.

Next to us are all sorts of distractions that would hope to allure us away from the great work we are called to do. It's so easy to step away from the build when you see the end in view. A quick rest stop won't hurt, we think.

Say 'No' to the plains of Ono.

Quote to consider
The temptation to quit will be greatest just before you are about to succeed. Chinese proverb

Questions to answer
What are the plains of Ono to you? What false promises are they tempting you with?

A rock to build with
Be wary of false delights.

30. When God is at work

So the wall was finished in the twenty-fifth day of Elul, in fifty-two days. When all our enemies heard of it, all the nations that were around us were afraid, and were much cast down in their own eyes; for they perceived that this work was worked of our God. Moreover in those days the nobles of Judah sent many letters to Tobiah, and Tobiah's letters came to them. For there were many in Judah sworn to him, because he was the son-in-law of Shecaniah the son of Arah; and his son Jehohanan had taken the daughter of Meshullam the son of Berechiah as wife. Also they spoke of his good deeds before me, and reported my words to him. Tobiah sent letters to put me in fear. Nehemiah 6:15-19

Some of the most annoying little sayings are 'An old dog can't learn new tricks', 'A leopard can't change its spots' and 'A tiger can't change its stripes'. They imply that it is impossible to change, that we are doomed to be always the same.

Here is the good news. We're not an old dog, a leopard or a tiger. We are capable of change. The brain can change and adapt and learn new things. We are not doomed to always repeat the same old behaviours that may have plagued us for a lifetime.

Nehemiah and the people of Jerusalem have finished the wall. Fifty two days ago they were a people covered in shame and under the domination of others. Something quite miraculous had happened in those seven and a half weeks. A new identity, community and strength had grown so much so that those enemies that had been plaguing them were now the ones who were feeling shame and living in fear. They could see that this work could not have been done just by the people, but that the people had God next to them.

This incredible change for Jerusalem happened because there was a great love sweeping through the city. God's love inspired the community to change and build.

'Next to them' people grow and change through God's love entering into every moment of their lives.

Quote to consider

Where there is great love there are always miracles. Willa Cather

Questions to answer

Do you think you are like that 'Old dog who can't learn new tricks'? Have you confined others to being 'Leopards who can't change their spots'? Does God view you and others in this way?

A rock to build with
The 'and next to them' God can accomplish the seemingly impossible.

31. Gates and Doors

Now when the wall was built, and I had set up the doors, and the porters and the singers and the Levites were appointed, I put my brother Hanani, and Hananiah the governor of the fortress, in charge of Jerusalem; for he was a faithful man, and feared God above many. I said to them, "Don't let the gates of Jerusalem be opened until the sun is hot; and while they stand guard, let them shut the doors, and you bar them: and appoint watches of the inhabitants of Jerusalem, everyone in his watch, with everyone near his house." Nehemiah 7:1-3

Charlie was the friendliest guy I have ever known. He would welcome anyone into his home, serve them a coffee and make sure they knew that they were valued. Most people were respectful of Charlie's hospitality, but some weren't. Some came in and stole from him, abused him and left him robbed of dignity. Some were friends of Charlie, adding value to him; while others were robbers stealing something of who he was.

The wall of Jerusalem was built, but the inner security and strength were only as good as the ability to control who came in and out of the city. Doors and gates needed to be built.

There was a difference between a gate and a door. A gate is able to be opened from both the outside and the inside. A gate is free passage, but with limited restriction. A door is a different matter. This is something that could only be opened and closed from the inside. On the inside, the door is bolted and barred. Access is controlled from the inside.

There are some people who we do not allow into our lives. Perhaps we let them relate to us to some degree but no further. Trust has not been established yet to allow them further into the city of our hearts. We set up guards to watch for them; we bolt the door, lock it and maybe have vicious guard dogs to ward them off.

Others, because of the trust we have built up, we allow in. Intimacy can be broken down to 'In-to-me-see'. We allow those few and precious people to come in and eat with us, to commune together and be the soul mates we feel safe with.

Quote to consider
The most important distinction anyone can ever make in their life is between who they are as an individual and their connection with others. Anné Linden[19]

Questions to answer
Who do you let into your inner world and who do you have a bolted door to, and why?

A rock to build with
When you value yourself you will know your gates and doors.

---

[19] Anné Linden, Boundaries in Human Relationships: How to Be Separate and Connected

Conclusion

Charlie was the type of guy that didn't say much. I knew something about his background and it was shocking to hear of his abuse. Self-mutilation scars were evident for all to see. He kept a happy face on the outside but inside was a deeply hurt and anxious man.

He wore this baseball cap with embroidered words 'Shit Happens'. It offended some of the more religious fundamentalist friends he had, but I could see that he was making a profound statement. Shit happens. Walls get destroyed, abuse happen, and trauma hits the heart. It may have happened but Charlie wouldn't let it define him.

God was up to something good in Charlie's life - resurrection rebuilding. With a collective group of rebuilders, he started to move from broken to built. He helped others too. He helped me with his embroidered hat.

This is your journey too - join with a few others and build.

Keep coming back to the little devotionals. Share them with your fellow builders and keep building 'next to them' relationships.

ABOUT THE AUTHOR

Barry Pearman lives in Auckland New Zealand and has a
deep passion is
to empower people with Mental Illnesses to find recovery
and
hope.

Barry writes about Mental health and Spiritual Formation
on his
website Turning the Page.

In former years he has had roles as a Mental
Health Support Worker and then as a Community
Chaplain pastoring
people with Major Mental Illnesses.

Read more at https://turningthepage.info/.